Colorado's Great Outdoors

Celebrating 20 Years of Lottery-Funded Lands

Photography by John Fielder

Published in Cooperation with the Great Outdoors Colorado Trust Fund

JOHN FIELDER PUBLISHING

Silverthorne, Colorado

GEORGE BEARDSLEY

This book is dedicated to the memory of George Beardsley, a member of the first Great Outdoors Colorado Board and key member of the coalition that helped successfully pass the GOCO ballot initiative. His love of Colorado, keen financial sense, and dry wit helped make GOCO one of the most successful organizations in the state. George was also selfless and would think it remiss not to thank all those first Board members who breathed life into the will of the voters to see Colorado's outdoors protected and enhanced for our children.

ISBN: 978-0-9860004-2-3

PHOTOGRAPHS COPYRIGHT: Great Outdoors Colorado Trust Fund and John Fielder, 2012. All rights reserved.
TEXT COPYRIGHT: Great Outdoors Colorado Trust Fund, 2012. All rights reserved.
COVER AND TEXT DESIGN: Rebecca Finkel, F + P Graphic Design
EDITOR: Deb Olson

PUBLISHED BY:
John Fielder Publishing
P.O. Box 26890
Silverthorne, Colorado 80497

Printed in China

FRONTISPIECE PHOTOGRAPHS:
Clear Creek Canyon, Jefferson County
Cline Ranch, South Park, Park County
Spruce Mountain Open Space, Douglas County
TITLE PAGE: Focus Ranch, Routt County
PAGE 8: Plains Conservation Center, Arapahoe County

COVER PHOTOGRAPH: Sunset, Cherry Creek State Park, Arapahoe County

For more information about books and calendars published by John Fielder and John Fielder Publishing, please contact your local bookstore, web retailer, John Fielder's Colorado Gallery (303-744-7979), or visit **johnfielder.com**. Book resellers please contact Books West distributors at **bookswest.net**.

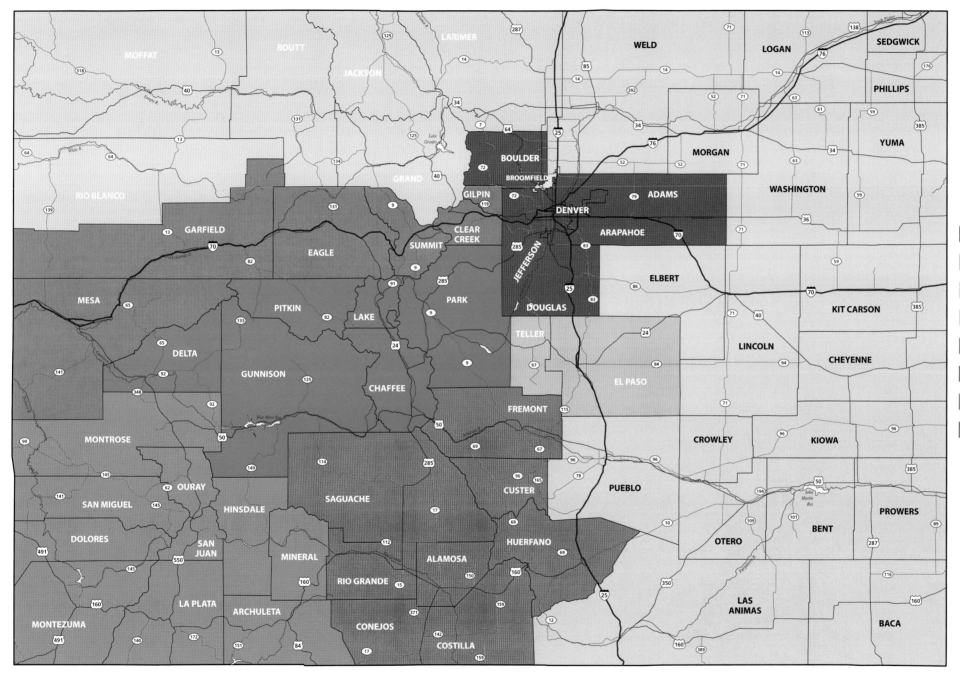

CONTENTS

FOREWORD

One of my life's greatest gifts is that five generations ago my ancestors settled in Colorado and built a family ranch in the heart of the San Luis Valley. I was fortunate to grow up in this remarkable place where citizens share an ethic that land, water and wildlife are worthy of our stewardship.

When I served as Director of the Colorado Department of Natural Resources, I continued to witness the importance of the outdoors to people throughout the state. Colorado's outdoors provide recreational resources, and opportunities to experience wildlife and natural wonders. The outdoors are also vital to Colorado's economy as they foster tourism and spending on recreation, and make Colorado a place where companies and their employees want to live.

While I have been blessed with numerous opportunities in life, including serving as Colorado's Attorney General and U.S. Senator, one of my proudest accomplishments remains helping to enact the Great Outdoors Colorado Trust Fund. This program is unique in the nation and it serves as a testament to Coloradans' love of the outdoors.

In the face of unprecedented growth that saw prime agricultural lands, wildlife habitat, natural areas, and corridors between communities lost to development—and recreational areas unable to keep pace with demand—Coloradans took action and voted to make funding for the outdoors via GOCO part of the Colorado Constitution.

I recall traveling across the state as the first chair of the Great Outdoors Colorado Board to talk with people and hear their aspirations for their communities and for Colorado's outdoors. Whether helping to preserve open space and river corridors, enabling a town to build its first playground, improving and expanding our state parks system, growing a network of trails, or protecting wildlife, GOCO continues to help realize these aspirations. In the 20 years since its passage, the benefit of GOCO dollars is evident in urban, suburban and rural areas across the state. The Yampa River in northwest Colorado has been the centerpiece of agricultural land preservation, a new state park, state wildlife areas and an expanded trails network. Prime agricultural lands and 12 miles of the Rio Grande River have been protected through conservation easements, 10 of which are adjacent to other protected lands including the Rio Grande National Forest and the Monte Vista National Wildlife Refuge. The South Platte River Corridor, running through Denver, Arapahoe and Adams counties, has been transformed into trails, parks and improved wildlife habitat, as well as an area that allows urban children to experience and learn about the wonders of the outdoors.

These are just a few examples of why, without GOCO funding, this state would look much different today, and Coloradans' aspirations would have taken decades to achieve if they were achieved at all.

Another one million people could be added to the state's population in the next 10 years. I am very proud to say that through GOCO's continued work, and that of its many partners, we can preserve the Colorado we love for our children. GOCO has already left an indelible mark on Colorado's landscape and her people in its first 20 years. I am enthused about its continuing work for many more decades.

—KEN SALAZAR
United States Secretary of the Interior

Peanut Lake sunrise, Crested Butte, Gunnison County

INTRODUCTION

This book features images from my two-year project to photograph Colorado's wildlife, park, river, trail, and open space heritage, the work of Great Outdoors Colorado (GOCO) from 1993 to 2012. It is the companion publication to *Colorado's Great Outdoors: Lottery-Funded Parks, Trails, Wildlife Areas & Open Spaces,* a guide to hundreds of these places. The photographs in this book are what I consider to be the best images from my portfolio from the perspective of scenery, light, and composition. It features mostly ranches and county open spaces rather than more accessible municipal facilities such as ball fields, skate parks, and children's playgrounds. The many working ranches depicted have benefited from GOCO grants because of the significant wildlife habitat they provide. They are not accessible to the public, but instead remain in private ownership. This will be the first time many people have been able to see these lands. The book is divided into eight geographic regions and the captions under each photograph include the county in which the land is located.

The Origin of Great Outdoors Colorado

To understand the origins of the Great Outdoors Colorado Trust Fund, you first must understand the history of Colorado Lottery proceeds. When Coloradans voted to create a lottery in 1980, the issue put to voters was: "An amendment to Section 2 of Article XVIII of the Constitution of the State of Colorado, authorizing the establishment of a state-supervised lottery with the net proceeds—unless otherwise authorized by statute—allocated to the conservation trust fund of the state for distribution to municipalities and counties for park, recreation, and open space purposes." This measure passed with 59.8% of voters in favor. The Colorado Lottery was implemented on July 1, 1982 when the General Assembly passed Senate Bill 119. The distribution formula in that bill was different than the ballot language. It directed that 40 percent of net proceeds be allocated to the Conservation Trust Fund to support local parks, recreation, and open space projects; 10 percent be allocated to state parks and outdoor recreation programs; and the remaining net proceeds be allocated to state capital construction projects.

Fast forward to 1990: Ken Salazar, the newly-appointed executive director of the Colorado Department of Natural Resources, beseeched Governor Roy Romer to create a committee that would explore ways to invest in Colorado's natural heritage. While considering the inconsistency between the Lottery proceeds distribution formula and the intent of voters, the committee of interested citizens also looked at many revenue sources that could benefit Colorado's outdoor resources, including sales and property taxes. The committee ultimately recommended to Governor Romer that the 50 percent of Lottery proceeds allocated for capital construction projects be redirected to benefit local parks, recreation, and open space projects, as Coloradans had originally intended.

The Governor agreed, but the General Assembly refused to refer a measure to the people, so an effort was launched to gather enough signatures to place a citizens' initiative on the 1992 ballot. The initiative passed handily and gave the former state capital construction money to the Great Outdoors Colorado Trust Fund, with the stipulation that it be capped at $35 million per year, adjusted annually for the cost of living index, and that any leftover money be returned to the state's general fund (this has subsequently changed so that leftover money now goes to school capital construction). The ballot measure also reaffirmed that 40 percent of Lottery proceeds go to the Conservation Trust Fund and 10 percent to Colorado's state parks.

About Great Outdoors Colorado
The Mission

Great Outdoors Colorado's mission is to help preserve, protect, enhance, and manage the state's wildlife, park, river, trail, and open space heritage.

The Colorado Constitution requires GOCO to allocate its proceeds to four areas in substantially equal portions over time:

- "Investments in the wildlife resources of Colorado through the Colorado Division of Wildlife (as of 2011, the Colorado Division of Parks and Wildlife), including the protection and restoration of crucial wildlife habitats, appropriate programs for maintaining Colorado's diverse wildlife heritage, wildlife watching, and educational programs about wildlife and wildlife environment."

- "Investments in the outdoor recreation resources of Colorado through the Colorado Division of Parks and Outdoor Recreation (as of 2011, the Colorado Division of Parks and Wildlife), including the State Parks system, trails, public information and environmental education resources, and water for recreational facilities."

- "Competitive grants to the Colorado Division of Parks and Wildlife, and to counties, municipalities, or other political subdivisions of the state, or non-profit land conservation organizations, to identify, acquire, and manage open space and natural areas of statewide significance."
- "Competitive matching grants to local governments or other entities which are eligible for distributions from the Conservation Trust Fund, to acquire, develop, or manage open lands and parks."

From these four funding areas, GOCO has developed a variety of grant programs.

Accomplishments

Since awarding its first grants in 1994 through 2011, GOCO has committed more than $715 million for nearly 3,500 projects in all 64 counties throughout the state. GOCO dollars have helped:

- protect more than 837,000 acres of open space in perpetuity, including land along river corridors and in mountain valleys; land for wildlife habitat; agricultural land; land in the heart of cities; land that separates communities; and land that buffers state and local parks from encroaching development.
- create or enhance 1,172 community park and outdoor recreation areas, including skate parks, ball fields, and playgrounds.
- assist the Colorado Division of Parks and Wildlife in acquiring and enhancing wildlife habitat; improving species' status to delist or prevent them from being listed under the federal Threatened and Endangered Species Program; providing wildlife viewing opportunities; enhancing facilities at existing state parks; buying land and providing facilities at new state parks; acquiring buffers to protect parks from encroaching development; and providing youth education.
- build or restore nearly 720 miles of trail.
- enable thousands of teenagers and young adults to participate in the Colorado Youth Corps Association.
- offer consistent, current and complete information about the status and trends of open space lands throughout Colorado via the state's first inventory of open space. The inventory provides detailed maps with comprehensive attributes listed for each parcel of land.

The GOCO Amendment created a diverse Board to oversee distribution of funds and represent all corners of the state. It consists of two members from each congressional district, two representatives designated by the Division of Parks and Wildlife Commission, and the Executive Director of the Department of Natural Resources. GOCO Board members are appointed by the Governor, subject to the consent of the Senate, for terms of four years. At least two members must reside west of the Continental Divide, and at least one must represent agricultural interests.

GOCO's staff and outside experts evaluate each grant application. The staff then submits recommendations to the GOCO Board, which makes all final funding decisions. GOCO continues to keep administrative expenses low: Its operating expenses, Board expenses, and capital investments combined remain less than 4 percent of total revenues received.

GOCO cannot and does not buy land, but makes grants to local governments, land trusts, and the Colorado Division of Parks and Wildlife. These entities either purchase land outright or work with landowners to place conservation easements on their properties.

When landowners agree to place a conservation easement on their property, they sell the development rights to their land, not the land itself. This provides landowners with a stream of income and enables them to continue agricultural production while preventing the land from ever being developed. The land remains privately-owned and on the state's tax rolls. Conservation easements placed on agricultural land protect important wildlife habitat and scenic views.

GOCO and Colorado Children

GOCO's investments in Colorado are visible in communities throughout the state. However, the organization's soundest investment—and one that offers the greatest return—just may be its continued investment in Colorado's children and young adults. Statewide, school-based and education-related projects have garnered nearly $20 million in GOCO/Lottery funds over the years. GOCO-funded projects range from vital school facilities and resources like playgrounds, outdoor classrooms, running tracks, ball fields, and tennis courts to educational programming offered through the Division of Parks and Wildlife. GOCO-funded environmental education programs at various state parks have been recognized for excellence by the Colorado Alliance for Environmental Education.

GOCO was instrumental in starting the Colorado Youth Corps Association (CYCA), which creates opportunities for young people to participate in high-quality youth corps statewide. Participants construct trails, remove weeds, and help remove beetle kill while receiving environmental education and developing an appreciation for Colorado's outdoors. With approximately 1,800 annual participants, CYCA received $1 million from GOCO in 2011 to continue its work in state parks and on wildlife habitat, and expand work for local governments and land trusts.

While GOCO has long recognized the importance of connecting youth and families with the outdoors, this was reaffirmed when the GOCO Board adopted a revised strategic plan in April 2010. The result of an extensive process that included 14 public meetings held throughout the state, GOCO's Strategic Plan identifies priorities and initiatives for the GOCO Board, and guides GOCO's grant-making and investments for the next five to 10 years—

all within the confines of the GOCO Amendment to the Constitution. "Youth, Families and the Outdoors" was among the top three funding priorities identified in the Strategic Plan, with the specific goal of increasing participation by youth and families in all areas of GOCO's mission.

To help accomplish this, GOCO is currently leading efforts to identify partnerships and available funding sources for providing accessible outdoor recreation for youth and families, as well as environmental education, stewardship training, and youth employment opportunities on public lands. GOCO recently awarded funds to Larimer County for a pilot project that will analyze the ties youth and families in the area have to the natural environment. The county will work with various stakeholders to explore existing nature programming and how families use it, available outdoor spaces and facilities, and the barriers to getting Larimer County youth and families connected to nature. The county will then map these gaps to create a visual model for future planning.

GOCO is taking its commitment to youth and families to the next level by using the Larimer County pilot as a template for similar studies across Colorado. Identifying statewide gaps in outdoor resources and programming for children and families will enable GOCO to invest strategically and ensure that everyone has access to Colorado's great outdoors regardless of how and where they live.

Moving Forward

Colorado's record of protecting its natural resources and promoting recreational opportunities for residents and visitors is impressive. In the 1960s and 1970s, foresighted citizens recognized the extraordinary quality of life offered by Colorado's plains, mountains, and rivers—and their appeal to people from around the world. The City and County of Denver— through the creation of its park system—and the City of Boulder, Boulder County, and Jefferson County were pioneers, not just in Colorado but nationally, in dedicating funding to protect open space, create parks, and build trails for its residents. The birth of GOCO accelerated this tradition by funding and bolstering the plans of these and so many other counties, cities, and towns, many of which have also voted to dedicate local resources to the outdoors. And, Colorado is the only state in the nation that commits virtually all of its lottery profits to protecting its natural heritage.

There were 2.2 million Colorado residents when I arrived here in 1969. By 1980, there were 2.9 million of us, and by 1990, 3.3 million people had discovered our wonderful state. These numbers seemed not to impose on our opportunity to enjoy solitude. Then the floodgates opened. One million people moved here in the decade of the 1990s, and another 700,000 after that. As of the publication of this book, there are about five million Colorado residents, most of whom use our local parks, trails, wildlife areas, state parks, and county open spaces. GOCO's birth in 1992 couldn't have been more timely. Will people stop moving to Colorado? Of course not. In the future, we could easily gain another 700,000 residents per decade, which would make eight million of us by 2050. These numbers will arguably stress the capacity of our parks and trails, and compromise the quality of the experience. Therefore, we must continue to invest in Colorado's natural heritage if we are to preserve our unique quality of life.

North Table Mountain Park Open Space,
Jefferson County

For most of my career, I have photographed Colorado's public lands. I have spent the last four years of my life photographing municipal and county open space, and privately-owned working ranches. At the same time, I have learned about ecology and the relationship of all living things, including us humans, with the natural environment. The integrity of biodiversity increases proportionally with the size of the land mass protected. Connecting private lands contiguously to public lands simultaneously enhances our outdoor opportunities and preserves nature. GOCO facilitates this process.

When one studies societies that survive over time and those that do not, it's clear that those that protect their forests, water supplies, and, in general, the natural environment, last the longest. They also have the most robust and sustainable economies. By investing in the outdoors, Colorado guarantees itself a steady stream of well-educated residents, relatively high-paying jobs, and billions of dollars in annual tourism revenues. Costs like medical care go down, too. People who play outdoors are healthier physically and psychologically. In nature, we refer to creatures that depend upon one another, that gain a mutual benefit from one another, as symbiotic. It is clear that in Colorado our economy and our ecology are symbiotic. It is my hope that the work of Great Outdoors Colorado will never end.

—JOHN FIELDER
Nature Photographer, GOCO Board Member 1993–2000

Clear Creek Canyon, Jefferson County

Opposite: Hildebrand Ranch Open Space, Jefferson County

South Platte Park, Arapahoe County

Nelson Ranch, Douglas County

Prairie Canyon Ranch, Douglas County

Palmer Divide Ranch, Douglas County

Next page: Bear Creek Lake Park, Jefferson County

Above: Cherry Creek State Park, Arapahoe County

Opposite: South Platte River sunrise, Larson Farm, Adams County

Nelson Ranch, Douglas County

Cherry Creek Regional Trail, Centennial, Arapahoe County

Standley Lake Regional Park, Jefferson County

Opposite: North Table Mountain Park Open Space, Jefferson County

Elaine T. Valente Open Space, Adams County

Roxborough State Park, Douglas County

Plains Conservation Center, Arapahoe County

Old Stone House Environmental Education Center, Adams County

Sand Creek, Sand Creek Regional Greenway, Denver County

Opposite: Castlewood Canyon State Park, Douglas County

Barr Lake State Park, Adams County

Bluff Lake Nature Center, Denver County

Spruce Mountain Open Space, Douglas County

Opposite: Two Ponds National Wildlife Refuge, Jefferson County

Next page: Cherry Creek State Park, Arapahoe County

Eldorado Canyon State Park, Boulder County

Left: Centennial Cone Park Open Space, Jefferson County

Coal Creek Trail, Boulder County

Parkfield Lake Park, Denver County

Rock Creek Farm, Carolyn Holmberg Preserve, Boulder County

Opposite: Chatfield State Park, Jefferson and Douglas Counties

Stone Ranch, Teller County

Opposite: Section 16 Open Space, El Paso County

Sinton Pond Open Space, Colorado Springs, El Paso County

Centennial Trail, Woodland Park, El Paso County

Gaffney Ranch, Teller County

Red Rock Canyon Open Space, El Paso County

Opposite: Markus Ranch, Teller County

Aiken Canyon, El Paso County

Fountain Creek Regional Trail, El Paso County

EASTERN PLAINS

Apishapa Ranch, Otero County

Opposite: Centennial Valley State Wildlife Area, Weld County

Red Top Ranch, Pueblo and Huerfano Counties

Winship Six Ranches, Cheyenne County

Above and Opposite: Lake Pueblo State Park, Pueblo County

Middle Bijou Creek Ranch, Arapahoe and Elbert Counties

South Republican State Wildlife Area, Yuma County

Opposite: Elliott State Wildlife Area, Morgan County

Fox Ranch, Yuma County

Sangre de Cristo Mountains, Trinidad Lake State Park, Las Animas County

Next page: St. Vrain State Park, Weld County

Fireweed wildflowers, Colorado State Forest State Park, Jackson County

Opposite: Lupine wildflowers, Carpenter Ranch, Routt County

Poudre River, Three Bells Ranch II, Larimer County

Wenschhof Ranch State Habitat Area, Rio Blanco County

Yampa River, Chuck Lewis State Wildlife Area, Routt County

Opposite: Yampa River State Park, Routt County

Sunset, Iva Mae Ranch, Jackson County

Little Snake River sunrise, Focus Ranch, Routt County

Opposite: Pronghorn antelope, Soapstone Prairie Open Space, Larimer County

Medicine Bow Mountains, Five Card Draw Ranch, Larimer County

Opposite: Fossil Creek Reservoir Open Space Park, Larimer County

Knott Ranch, Routt County

Red Mountain Ranch Open Space, Larimer County

Elk, Wolf Mountain Ranch, Routt County

Salisbury Homestead Ranch, Routt County

Fraser River, Grand County

Opposite: Sylvan Dale Ranch, Larimer County

Next page: Yampa River State Park, Elkhead Reservoir, Moffat and Routt Counties

Coyte Ranch, Jackson County

Klinglesmith-Berryman State Habitat Area, Rio Blanco County

Lunney Mountain State Habitat Area, Rio Blanco County

Opposite: Cedar Mountain Trail, Moffat County

A flooded Yampa River, Loudy Simpson Park, Craig, Moffat County

Boyd Lake State Park, Larimer County

Hillsdale Nature Park, Berthoud, Larimer County

Opposite: Wolf-Taussig Ranch State Habitat Area, Grand County

I-70 Corridor

James M. Robb—Colorado River State Park, Island Acres, Mesa County

Opposite: Gates Ranch, Eagle County

Vega State Park, Mesa County

James M. Robb—Colorado River State Park, Island Acres, Mesa County

Bashore Open Space, Summit County

Opposite: Beaver Brook Watershed, Clear Creek County

Next page: Armstrong Orchard & Vineyard, Mesa County

Gore Range, Cow Camp Open Space, Summit County

Yurt, Sylvan Lake State Park, Eagle County

Jerome Park, Garfield and Pitkin Counties
Opposite: Nieslanik Ranch, Garfield County

Bair Ranch, Eagle County

Riverview Orchard & Vineyard, Mesa County

James M. Robb—Colorado River State Park, Connected Lakes, Mesa County

Van Loan Ranch, Mesa County

Opposite: Bashore Open Space, Summit County

Rock Bottom Ranch, Garfield and Eagle Counties

Clear Creek, Oxbow Parcel, Clear Creek County

Crystal Valley Trail in Pitkin County

Opposite: Scarlet gilia wildflowers, Guerrieri Ranch, Gunnison County

Tarryall Creek in South Park, Tarryall Notch Ranch, Park County

Tomichi Creek, Cross Bar Ranch, Gunnison County

Next page: Mosquito Range tarn, Moyer 45 Ranch, Lake County

Arkansas Headwaters Recreation Area, Chaffee County

Opposite: Peanut Lake sunrise, Crested Butte, Gunnison County

Cold Mountain Ranch, Pitkin County

Middle Fork South Platte River, Santa Maria Ranch, Park County

Mosquito Range sunset, Moyer 45 Ranch, Lake County

Opposite: East River, Guerrieri Ranch, Gunnison County

Collegiate Peaks of the Sawatch Range, Rafter 26 Ranch, Chaffee County

Kochevar Open Space, Crested Butte, Gunnison County

Roaring Fork River, Grange Family Ranch, Pitkin County

Opposite: Darien Ranch, Pitkin County

Wild iris wildflowers, Post Office Ranch, Chaffee County

Previous page: Elze Ranch, Gunnison County

Sunflowers, Filoha Meadows Open Space, Pitkin County

Droste-Seven Star Open Space, Pitkin County

Opposite: Davis Ranch, Gunnison County

Lower Loop Trail, Crested Butte, Gunnison County

Crawford State Park, Delta County

SOUTHERN COLORADO

Higel Ranch, Alamosa County

Opposite: Bison below the Sangre de Cristo Mountains, Medano-Zapata Ranch, Alamosa County

Cochetopa State Wildlife Area, Saguache County

McNeil Ranch, Rio Grande County

Gilmore Ranch, Alamosa County

Opposite: Dunn Ranch, Saguache County

Russell Lakes State Wildlife Area, Saguache County

Lathrop State Park, Huerfano County
Next page: Music Meadows Ranch, Wet Mountain Valley, Custer County

San Isabel Ranch, Wet Mountain Valley, Custer County

Opposite: Sunrise, Medano-Zapata Ranch, Alamosa County

Gilmore Ranch, Alamosa County

Home Lake State Wildlife Area, Rio Grande County

Mule deer, River Valley Ranch, Rio Grande County

Opposite: Vickerman Ranch, Sangre de Cristo Mountains, Custer County

Rio Grande, Rio Oxbow Ranch, Mineral County

Opposite: Lone Cone, Brumley Ranch, Dolores County

Bear Creek Canyon, San Miguel County

Opposite: Animas River Greenway, Durango, La Plata County

Reddert Ranch, San Juan Skyway Legacy project, Montezuma County

Dick White Ranch, San Juan Skyway Legacy project, Montezuma County

Sanburg Ranch, Montrose County

Opposite: Lone Mesa State Park, Dolores County

Ridgway State Park, Ouray County

Previous page: Molas Lake Park, San Juan County

Dan Noble State Wildlife Area, San Miguel County

RSL Ranch, Dolores County

Opposite: East Fork San Juan River, East Fork Ranch, Archuleta County

Kentucky Placer, San Miguel County

Overend Mountain Park, La Plata County

Top of the Pines Open Space, Ouray County

JOHN FIELDER

John Fielder has worked tirelessly to promote the protection of Colorado's ranches, open spaces, and wildlands during his 30-year career as a nature photographer. His photography has influenced people and legislation, earning him recognition including the Sierra Club's Ansel Adams Award in 1993 and, in 2011, the Aldo Leopold Foundation's first Achievement Award given to an individual.

He was a member of the 1990 committee appointed by Governor Roy Romer to explore ways in which to invest in protecting and enhancing Colorado's outdoor heritage, as well as a member of the citizen's committee that placed the Great Outdoors Colorado (GOCO) initiative on the 1992 ballot. He traveled the state that year to share his photographs of Colorado with interested people and organizations, and to speak on behalf of the measure that dedicates virtually all Colorado Lottery proceeds to recreation, open space and wildlife. In 1993, he was appointed by Governor Romer to the Great Outdoors Colorado Board, and served two four-year terms.

John approached the Great Outdoors Colorado Board in 2010 and beseeched it to consider celebrating GOCO's 20th anniversary in 2012 with the publication of a guide book, *Guide to Colorado's Great Outdoors: Lottery-Funded Parks, Trails, Wildlife Areas & Open Spaces,* and this picture book, *Colorado's Great Outdoors: Celebrating 20 Years of Lottery-Funded Lands,* depicting many of the places invested in by GOCO. The board partnered with him to photograph hundreds of county and city open spaces, wildlife habitat, state parks and wildlife areas, local and regional trails, and community parks, ball fields, and playgrounds. John drove 35,000 miles in less than two years from one end of Colorado to the other, and visited all of the state's 64 counties and practically every city and town, in order to complete the project. John also agreed to tour Colorado in 2012 and 2013 to present his photography and recount his impressions of GOCO's accomplishments, in dozens of venues across the state at events hosted by Colorado's land protection community.

John Fielder lives in Summit County, Colorado. He operates a fine art gallery, John Fielder's Colorado, in Denver's Art District on Santa Fe. He teaches photography workshops to adults and children. Information about John and his work can be found at **johnfielder.com**. Copies of all of his books and calendars, including these Great Outdoors Colorado books, can be ordered online, or by calling his gallery at 303-744-7979.